MW00933353

THE COLORING BOOK OF THE ART OF
MARSDEN HARTLEY

RICK KINSEL

LINE DRAWINGS
PAULA KINSEL

MERRELL
LONDON · NEW YORK

IN ASSOCIATION WITH

VILCEK
FOUNDATION

INTRODUCTION

The American artist Marsden Hartley (1877-1943) grew up a poor boy in a factory town in Maine, but he was full of creativity and imagination. By the time he was a young man, he had begun leading an artistic life of travel and adventure. Throughout his career as a painter, poet, and writer, Hartley loved being out in nature, and felt most at home there. Making art was so important to him that he lived very simply, and mostly alone. He wrote poems about his experiences and made paintings that helped him express his strong feelings. His paintings were sometimes of mountains, skies, or ocean waves, other times of animals, flowers, or people—but in all these artworks he felt that the use of color was extremely important. Perhaps you will experience similarly strong feelings as you color in this Marsden Hartley coloring book.

Hartley adored the wilderness of Maine, but his curiosity about the wider world never left him. As he grew older he traveled and explored many new places where nature pleased and excited him. And he traveled to look at art too. For a while he lived in New York, where he studied art, painted, met other artists, and visited museums. From there he continued on to Europe, where he lived first in Paris, then in Berlin. His painting expeditions in Europe took him to southern Germany, Austria, Italy, and the South of France. Back in the United States, he painted in some of its most beautiful places: on the beaches of Cape Cod, in the deserts of the American Southwest, and in the mountains and valleys of California. He even spent some time in Mexico. In each of these places, the colors that Hartley experienced were different—not just the colors of the landscape, but also those of the art made by the people who had lived there for many generations. He was fascinated

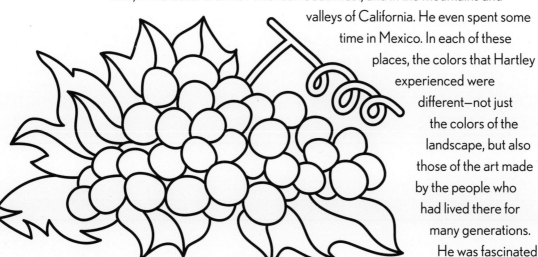

by the art of the ancient Egyptians, Aztecs, Native Americans, and Bavarian peasants. As a result, many of the patterns, motifs, and colors that occurred in their art became part of Hartley's art too.

Toward the end of his life, Hartley returned to Maine, the place of his birth. There, in a little cottage by the sea, he made some of his greatest paintings, featuring the skies, seas, and mountains, as well as fishermen, lumberjacks, and other people who lived so close to nature.

We hope that by looking at the paintings and drawings of Marsden Hartley—particularly at the colors of the paintings—you will be inspired to create your own works of art on the pages of this coloring book. You may feel as you do so that art, like nature, helps us know ourselves better: what we are thinking and feeling, what we care about, and what we love. That is just one of the ways in which art is so very important to us, and why we are so pleased to share it with you.

Rick Kinsel
President, The Vilcek Foundation

Atlantic Window in the New England Character
c. 1917
Oil on board
$31^5/_8$ x 25 in. (80.3 x 63.5 cm)

VILCEK COLLECTION, NEW YORK, 2005.04.01

Garmisch
October 13, 1933
Graphite on paper
10 1/8 x 7 1/8 in. (25.7 x 18.1 cm)

BATES COLLEGE MUSEUM OF ART, LEWISTON, MAINE,
MARSDEN HARTLEY MEMORIAL COLLECTION,
GIFT OF NORMA BERGER, 1955.1.28

[Study for *The Lost Felice*]
c. 1938
Black and brown ink with graphite
underdrawing on paper
10³⁄₈ x 7⁷⁄₈ in. (26.4 x 20 cm)

BATES COLLEGE MUSEUM OF ART, LEWISTON, MAINE,
MARSDEN HARTLEY MEMORIAL COLLECTION,
GIFT OF NORMA BERGER, 1955.1.44

Schiff
1915
Oil on canvas
39¾ x 31⅞ in. (101 x 81 cm)
VILCEK COLLECTION, NEW YORK, 2015.05.01

Tropical Fantasy
1936
Oil on canvas
20 1/8 x 24 1/8 in. (51.1 x 61.3 cm)
VILCEK COLLECTION, NEW YORK, VF2021.06.01

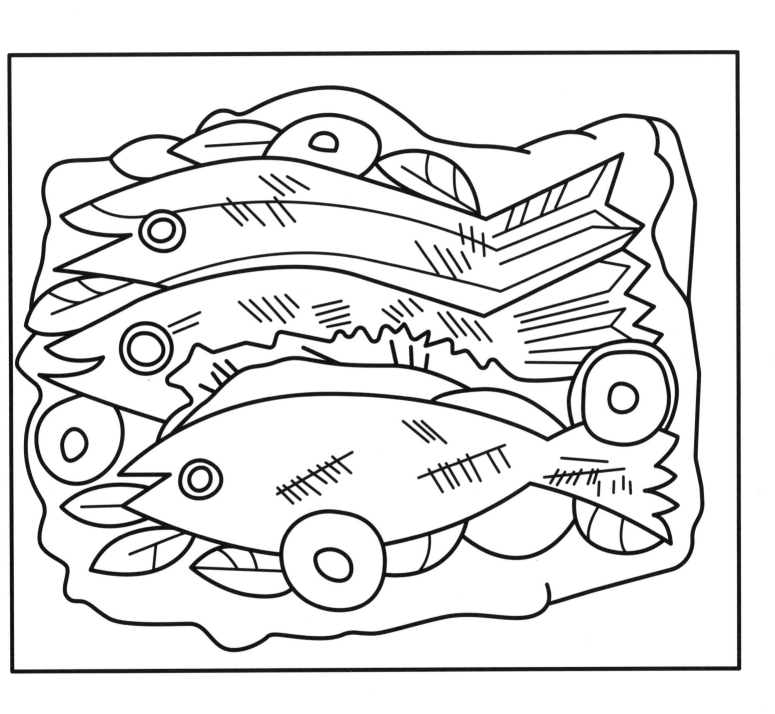

Camellias #1
1919–21
Oil on canvas
38½ x 21¾ in. (97.8 x 55.3 cm)

COLLECTION OF DAN PATTERSON

Symbol IV
c. 1913–14
Charcoal on paper
24½ x 18⅞ in. (62.2 x 47.9 cm)
VILCEK COLLECTION, NEW YORK, 2005.03.01

Mont Sainte-Victoire
c. 1927
Oil on canvas
20 x 24 in. (50.8 x 61 cm)
VILCEK COLLECTION, NEW YORK, 2007.06.01

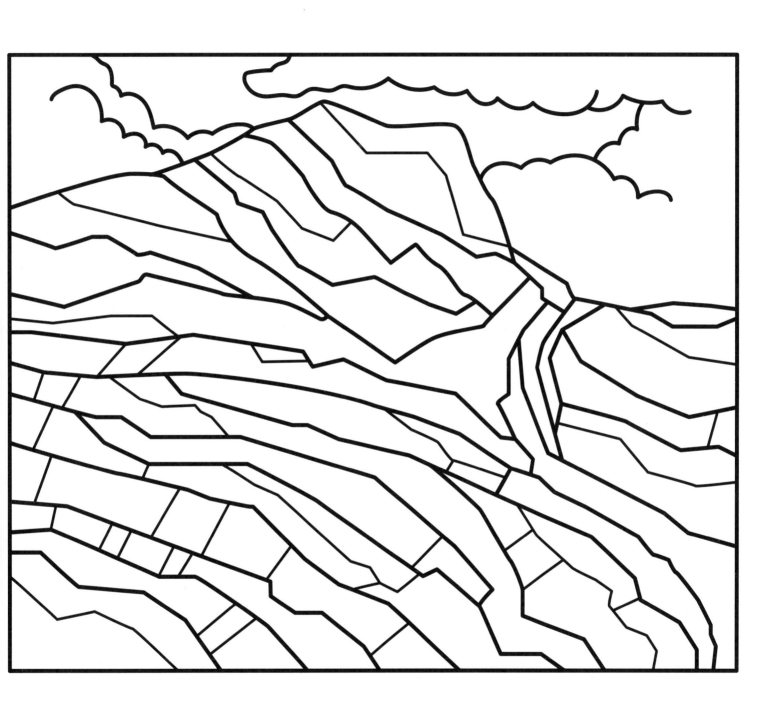

The Strong Man

c. 1923

Oil on canvas

13 x 32¼ in. (33 x 81.9 cm)

VILCEK COLLECTION, NEW YORK, 2006.03.05

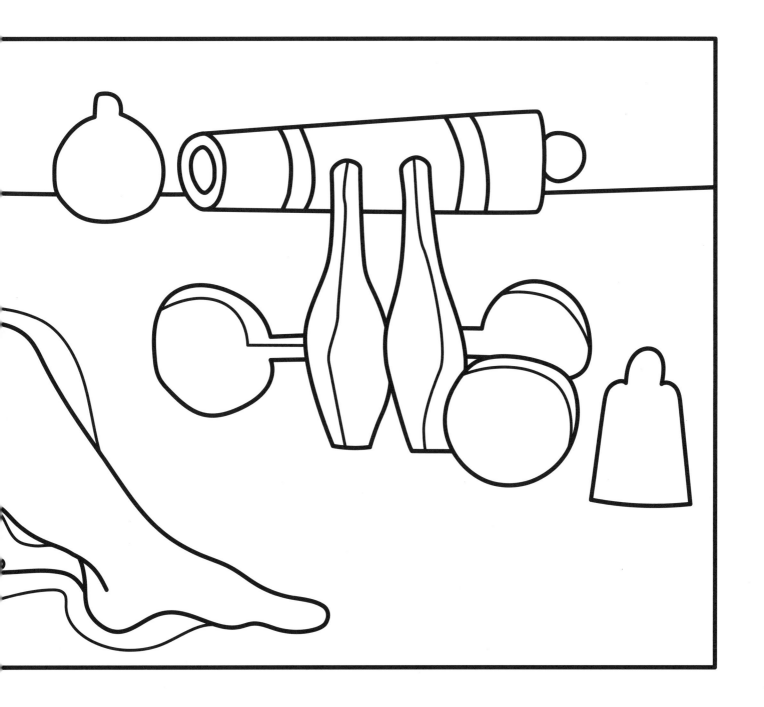

White Sea Horse
1942
Oil on Masonite
28 x 22 in. (71.1 x 55.9 cm)
VILCEK COLLECTION, NEW YORK, 2013.05.01

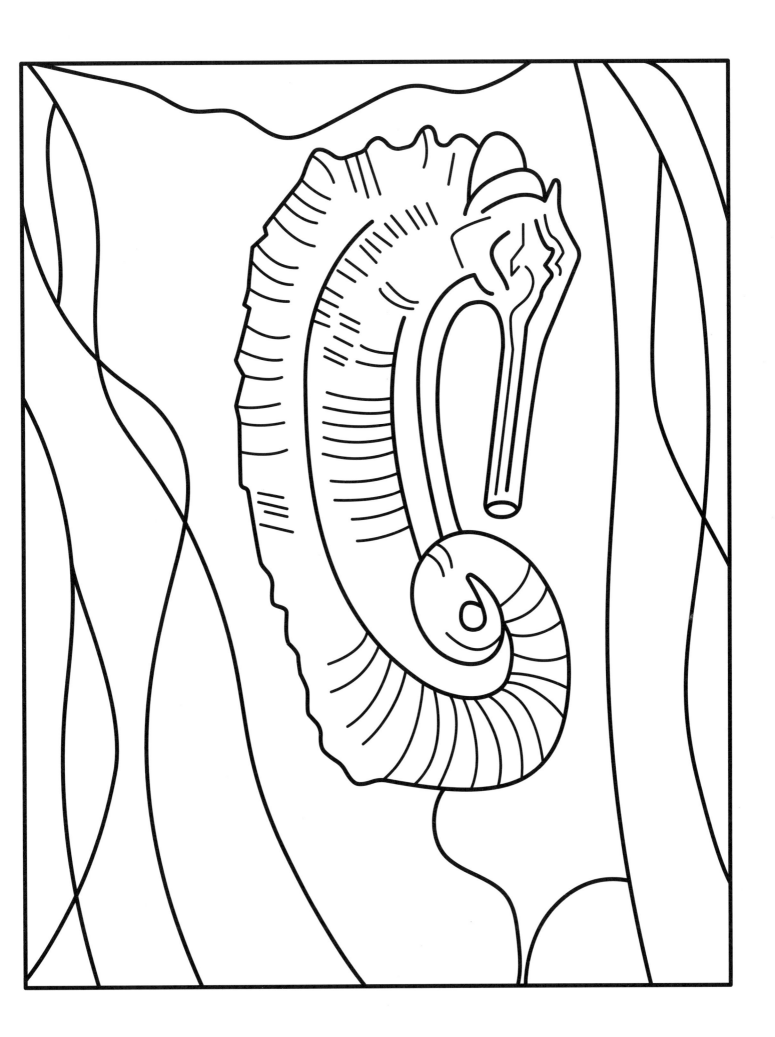

Untitled (Popocatépetl, Mexico)
c. 1932–33
Oil on canvas
28 x 30 in. (71.1 x 76.2 cm)
VILCEK COLLECTION, NEW YORK, 2021.01.01

Based on a portrait of Marsden Hartley
by an unknown photographer, 1908-1909,
in the Marsden Hartley Memorial Collection
at Bates College Museum of Art.

Museum Guard

n.d.
Black ink on paper
10¾ x 7 in. (27.3 x 17.8 cm)

BATES COLLEGE MUSEUM OF ART, LEWISTON, MAINE,
MARSDEN HARTLEY MEMORIAL COLLECTION,
GIFT OF NORMA BERGER, 1955.1.5

New Mexico Recollection
1923
Oil on canvas
12¾ x 32¼ in. (32.4 x 81.9 cm)
VILCEK COLLECTION, NEW YORK, 2008.06.01

Portrait Arrangement No. 2
1912-13
Oil on canvas
39½ x 31¾ in. (100.3 x 80.7 cm)
VILCEK COLLECTION, NEW YORK, 2005.09.01

[Study for *Fisherman's Family*]
c. 1936-43
Graphite on paper
10½ x 8 in. (26.7 x 20.3 cm)

BATES COLLEGE MUSEUM OF ART, LEWISTON, MAINE,
MARSDEN HARTLEY MEMORIAL COLLECTION,
GIFT OF NORMA BERGER, 1955.1.96

A Lady in Laughter
1919
Oil on board
23 x 18½ in. (58.4 x 47 cm)
COLLECTION OF CHRYSTINA AND JAMES PARKS

Indian Pottery
c. 1912
Oil on canvas
20¼ x 20¼ in. (51.4 x 51.4 cm)
VILCEK COLLECTION, NEW YORK, 2006.05.01

Berlin Series No. 1
1913
Oil on canvas board
18 x 15 in. (45.7 x 38.1 cm)

VILCEK COLLECTION, NEW YORK, 2012.01.01

Three Shells
c. 1941–43
Oil on board
22 x 28 in. (55.9 x 71.1 cm)
VILCEK COLLECTION, NEW YORK, 2012.04.02

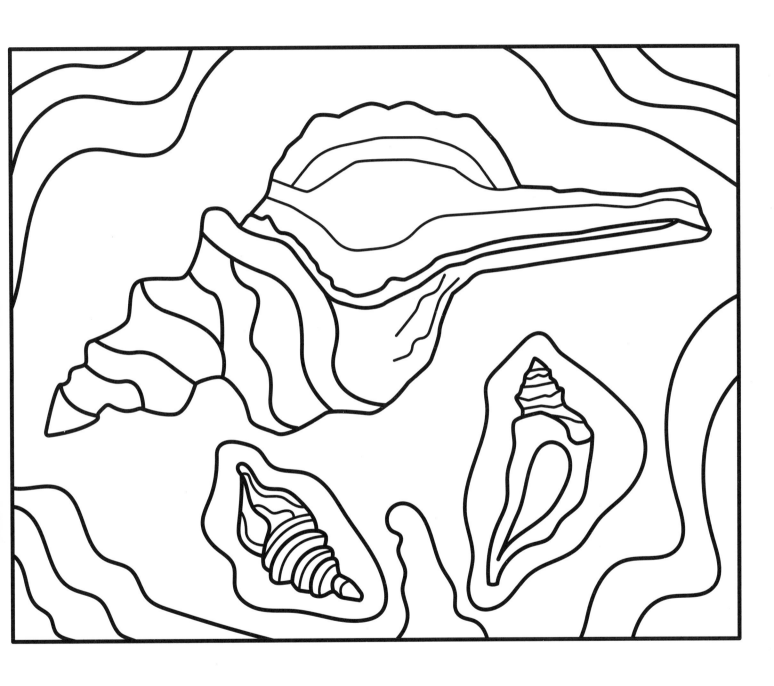

Grapes–Berlin
1922/23
Oil on canvas
10⅝ x 18⅜ in. (27 x 46.7 cm)

VILCEK COLLECTION, NEW YORK, 2005.05.01

New Mexico Landscape
c. 1923
Oil on canvas
17⅝ x 30⅛ in. (44.8 x 76.5 cm)
COLLECTION OF CHRYSTINA AND JAMES PARKS

Lost Country—Petrified Sand Hills
1932
Oil on Masonite
22¼ x 28½ in. (56.5 x 72.4 cm)
VILCEK COLLECTION, NEW YORK, 2018.01.01

Still Life—Pink Begonia
c. 1928-29
Oil on canvas
24 x 19½ in. (61 x 49.5 cm)
VILCEK COLLECTION, NEW YORK, 2020.01.01

The Waxenstein, Garmisch Partenkirchen
1933-34
Oil on cardboard
29¼ x 20¾ in. (74.3 x 52.7 cm)

VILCEK COLLECTION, NEW YORK, 2021.02.01

New Mexico Recollection #14
c. 1923
Oil on canvas
30 x 40 in. (76.2 x 101.6 cm)
VILCEK COLLECTION, NEW YORK, 2009.01.01

Roses for Seagulls that Lost their Way
1935-36
Oil on board
16 x 12 in. (40.6 x 30.5 cm)

VILCEK COLLECTION, NEW YORK, 2013.02.01

Symbol V
c. 1913-14
Charcoal on paper
24½ x 18⅞ in. (62.2 x 47.9 cm)
VILCEK COLLECTION, NEW YORK, 2005.03.02

Silence of High Noon–Midsummer
c.1907-1908
Oil on canvas
30½ x 30½ in. (77.5 x 77.5 cm)

VILCEK COLLECTION, NEW YORK, 2008.07.01

Autumn Landscape, Dogtown
1934
Oil on Masonite
20 x 27¾ in. (50.8 x 70.5 cm)
VILCEK COLLECTION, NEW YORK, 2012.04.01

MARSDEN
HARTLEY

First published 2022 by Merrell Publishers, London and New York

Merrell Publishers Limited
70 Cowcross Street
London EC1M 6EJ
merrellpublishers.com

in association with

Vilcek Foundation
21 East 70th Street
New York, NY 10021
vilcek.org

Text copyright © 2022 Vilcek Foundation
Illustrations copyright © 2022 Vilcek Foundation, with exceptions noted in captions. Photograph of colored pencils on cover: © iStock.com/ worldofstock
Design and layout copyright © 2022 Merrell Publishers Limited

All rights reserved. No part of this publication may be reproduced, stored in a retrieval system, or transmitted, in any form or by any means, electronic, mechanical, photocopying, recording, or otherwise, without the prior written permission of the publishers.

A catalogue record for this book is available from the Library of Congress.

British Library Cataloguing in Publication Data.
A catalogue record for this book is available from the British Library.

ISBN 978-1-8589-4708-2

Produced by Merrell Publishers Limited
Printed and bound in China

Note on captions: In those instances where Hartley did not title an artwork, a description is given in brackets.

Front cover: Detail of *Berlin Series No. 1*, 1913; see p. 41.
Back cover, left: Detail of *Untitled (Popocatépetl, Mexico)*, c. 1932–33; see p. 25.
Back cover, right, and page 1: Detail of *A Lady in Laughter*, 1919; see p. 37.
Page 2: Detail of *Grapes–Berlin*, 1922/23; see p. 45.
Page 3: Detail of *Tropical Fantasy*, 1936; see p. 13.
Above: Based on a photograph of Marsden Hartley by Man Ray, c. 1925, in the Marsden Hartley Memorial Collection at Bates College Museum of Art. © Man Ray 2015 Trust/DACS 2022.

Our thanks to Bates College Museum of Art, the Owings Gallery, Dan Patterson, Chrystina and James Parks, Jon Boos, and Justin Spring.

RICK KINSEL is President of the Vilcek Foundation.

PAULA KINSEL is an artist, graphic designer, and art director.